D0833887

BRICK CITY
LONDON

First published in the United States by
Lonely Planet Global Limited
www.lonelyplanetkids.com

First published in the United Kingdom by
Quarto Publishing plc in 2018

Copyright © 2018 Quarto Publishing plc

All rights reserved. No part of this publication may
be reproduced, stored in a retrieval system, or
transmitted in any form by any means, electronic,
mechanical, photocopying, recording, or otherwise,
except brief extracts for the purpose of review, without
the written permission of the publisher. Lonely Planet
and the Lonely Planet logo are trademarks of Lonely
Planet and are registered in the US Patent and
Trademark Office and in other countries.

Although the author and Lonely Planet have taken all
reasonable care in preparing this book, we make no
warranty about the accuracy or completeness of its
content and, to the maximum extent permitted,
disclaim all liability from its use.

2018 2019 2020 2021 / 10 9 8 7 6 5 4 3 2 1

ISBN: 978-1-78701-803-7

This book was conceived, designed and produced by
The Bright Press, an imprint of The Quarto Group
The Old Brewery
6 Blundell Street
London, N7 9BH
United Kingdom
T(0)20 7700 6700 F(0)20 7700 8066
www.quartoknows.com

Publisher: Mark Searle
Associate Publisher: Emma Bastow
Creative Director: James Evans
Art Director: Katherine Radcliffe
Managing Editor: Isheeta Mustafi
Senior Editor: Caroline Elliker
Project Editors: Alison Morris, Abi Waters
Design: Ali Adlington, Nina Tara

Printed and bound in the UAE

LEGO®, the LEGO® logo, the
Brick and Knob configuration
and the MINIFIGURE figurine are
trademarks and/or copyrights of
the LEGO® Group of Companies,
which does not sponsor,
authorise or endorse this book.

MIX
Paper from
responsible sources
FSC
www.fsc.org   **FSC® C004800**

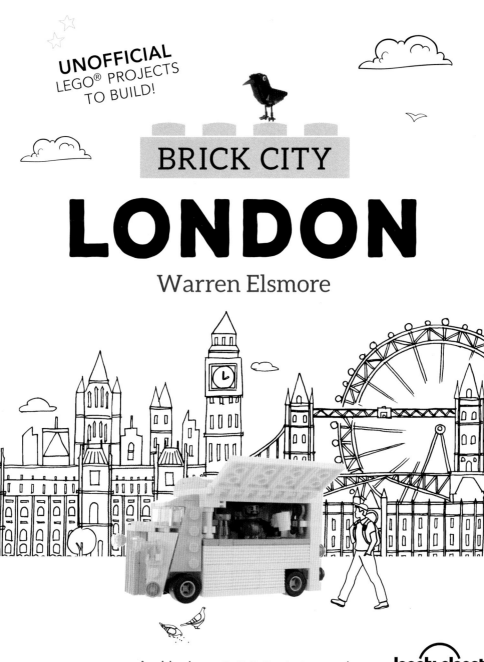

UNOFFICIAL LEGO® PROJECTS TO BUILD!

BRICK CITY

LONDON

Warren Elsmore

Leabharlanna Poiblí Chathair Baile Átha Cliath
Dublin City Public Libraries

lonely planet

Contents

There are 20 projects in this book to make yourself. Just look out for the brick symbol.

Welcome to Brick City
London

Read all about it! Read all about it! Come on up me old china plate (mate!) and welcome to the most iconic cities in the world – London. It's survived floods, fires, plagues and bombings and still come out on top. Londoners are made of tough stuff, just like the pigeons that flutter and bob along the busy streets. There's enough innovation to put a crackle in the air but it never drowns out a story of times gone by. Grand monuments stand alongside glowing West End theatres, charming cafés and a headline-grabbing royal family – and their palace.

Brick City London will take you on a whistle-stop tour of the city's most iconic attractions, from the Houses of Parliament to its handsome red phone boxes. Check out the amazing LEGO® models and scratch your head in wonder while you imagine the scent of frying fish and chips and the sound of Camden's punk rockers.

Want to know Big Ben's real name? How to become a Wimbledon ball girl/boy? Read on and discover

plenty of fun facts along the way. And you don't have to be a master builder to get involved.

Brick City London includes easy-to-follow instructions for 20 fun, unofficial LEGO® projects that you can make yourself.

Hold the city in the palm of your hand, from a fire-breathing City of London dragon to a cute red bus. Our expert author will guide you through the process, with tips on LEGO® building and sourcing unusual bricks. The Big Smoke awaits. Go and get stuck in!

TURN OVER TO SEE ALL THE BUILDABLES!

Brick Builds

Here's a quick visual guide to all the buildable LEGO® models in this book

REMEMBER! IF YOU SEE ME YOU CAN MAKE IT!

RED PHONE BOX PAGE 12

BOWLER HAT PAGE 16

ORB PAGE 34

STOCKS PAGE 39

10 DOWNING STREET PAGE 24

RAVEN PAGE 37

QUEEN'S GUARDS PAGE 64

THE CORONATION CHAIR PAGE 47

CITY OF LONDON DRAGON PAGE 53

FISH & CHIPS PAGE 79

THE BRITISH MUSEUM
PAGE 72

RED BUS
PAGE 104

CHINATOWN PAGE 92

SHERLOCK HOLMES
PAGE 123

FOOD TRUCK PAGE 84

ABBEY ROAD PAGE 106

WIMBLEDON
PAGE 113

UNDERGROUND TRAIN
PAGE 100

LORD'S CRICKET
GROUND PAGE 111

CANAL BOAT PAGE 118

TATE MODERN

The Tate Modern is one of London's most amazing spaces. Believe it or not, the main building used to be Bankside Power Station. Built using 4.2 million bricks and 200m (656ft) long, the Swiss architects Herzog and de Meuron scooped the prestigious Pritzker Architecture Prize for transforming the empty power station. The echoey Turbine Hall entrance showcases changing art installations by famous artists, from giant swings and slides to a crunchy carpet of ceramic sunflower seeds for visitors to walk over.

More than 60,000 works are on constant rotation at Tate Modern. The curators have famous works by Henri Matisse, Mark Rothko, Jackson Pollock and Damien Hirst all at their fingertips!

SPEEDY HUNTERS

Peregrine falcons are the fastest creatures on the planet. When they dive to attack their prey they can reach an incredible 320km/hr (199 mph). They like open spaces and cliffs, but they occasionally decide to live on city buildings. A few have chosen the Tate Modern as a place to hang out.

SOMETIMES BIRDWATCHERS SET UP OUTSIDE WITH THEIR BINOCULARS, HOPING FOR A PEREGRINE PEEK.

Red Phone Box

There's a surprising secret behind London's iconic red phone booths. Sir Giles Gilbert Scott, who first designed them in 1924, was inspired by the grave of architect Sir John Soane and his family in a churchyard in St Pancras. Scott used the tomb shape as a model for his booths, which were painted red to make them easy to spot.

Nowadays they only survive in conservation areas where they are often surrounded by crowds of selfie-happy tourists. Some have been sold and repurposed as cafés, libraries, and even mobile phone repair shops. Modern replacement 'booths' have high-speed wi-fi and touch-screen journey planners.

DEATH OF A PHONE BOOTH

A bent and shattered phone box appeared in Soho in 2006, lying sadly on the pavement with a pickaxe in its middle and a wound 'bleeding' red paint. It wasn't the victim of a phone box psychopath, however – this was guerrilla art by graffiti artist Banksy.

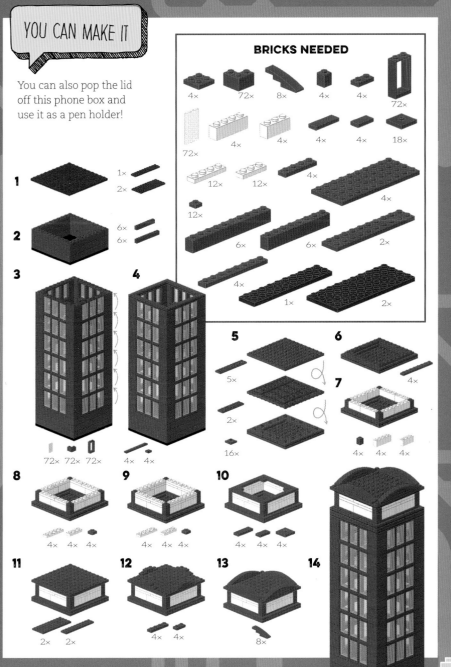

YOU CAN MAKE IT

You can also pop the lid off this phone box and use it as a pen holder!

BRICKS NEEDED

4× 72× 8× 4× 4× 72×

72× 4× 4× 4× 4× 18×

12× 12× 4×

12× 4×

6× 6× 2×

4× 1× 2×

1 1× 2×

2 6× 6×

3 72× 72× 72×

4 4× 4×

5 5× 2× 16×

6 4×

7 4× 4× 4×

8 4× 4× 4×

9 4× 4× 4×

10 4× 4× 4×

11 2× 2×

12 4× 4×

13 8×

14

THE GLOBE THEATRE

TO BE, OR NOT TO BE...

Britain's most famous playwright, William Shakespeare, lived and worked in London roughly 400 years ago. One of the theatres where his plays were performed was the Globe, which stood on the southern bank of the River Thames. Today there's a modern reconstruction close to the original site. The cheapest tickets are for the 'groundlings', who stand in front of the stage.

NO FAKES

Shakespearean actors used props such as real swords, which could cause nasty accidents onstage. In a stage fight actors wore sheeps' bladders filled with animal blood under their costumes, ready to give the illusion of a mortal wound.

LADS IN DISGUISE

Women weren't allowed on stage in Shakespeare's time, so the female parts were played by boys. There was stiff competition for the best parts, but once they grew and their voices broke, there was no guarantee they could carry on.

PANTS ON FIRE

In 1613, the Globe went up in flames during a performance of Shakespeare's Henry VIII. A cannon used as a prop misfired, setting fire to the roof. Nobody was hurt except a man who had to put out his burning breeches with a bottle of ale!

Each stage pillar is a whole oak tree. Over 1,000 were used to build the new Globe.

BOWLER HAT

Welcome to 1950s London where businessmen wearing bowler hats flow over London Bridge every morning. Founded in the capital in 1765, Lock & Co is the oldest hat shop in the world and even makes headgear by royal appointment. Lock & Co was the original inventor of the bowler hat, or 'Coke' (pronounced 'cook'), designed in 1849 as a commission for nobleman Edward Coke who wanted to protect his gamekeeper's heads from low-hanging branches when they were riding through the estate. Since then they have made bowlers for many famous customers, from Sir Winston Churchill to Charlie Chaplin.

In the James Bond film *Goldfinger*, the baddie, Oddjob, throws a razor-edged bowler hat at his enemies as a weapon. The original prop was later sold at auction for £62,000 ($83,600).

THE COKE CELEBRATED ITS 150TH ANNIVERSARY IN 1999

CELEBRITY CUSTOMERS WERE ASKED TO CUSTOMISE THEIR OWN HATS

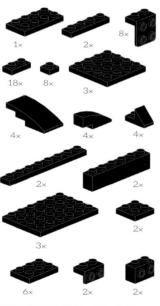

BRICKS NEEDED

1×   2×   8×

18×   8×   3×

4×   4×   4×

2×   2×

3×   2×

6×   2×   2×

Make a bowler hat fit for a prime minister with these easy instructions.

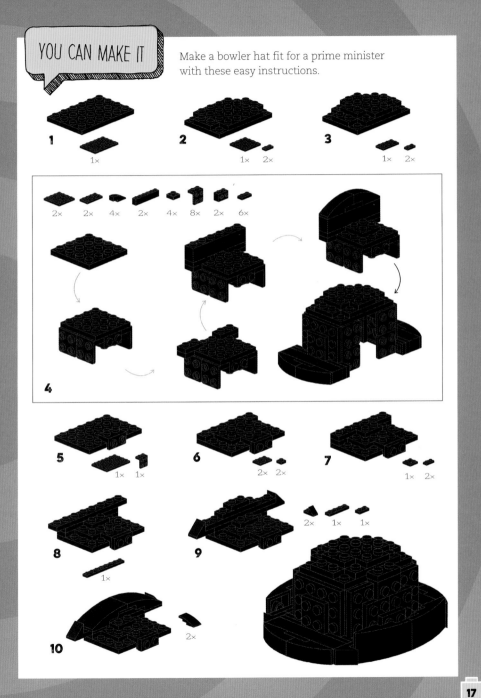

OXO TOWER

This prime spot on London's South Bank housed a power station until it was bought by the company that made OXO stock cubes – the Liebig Extract of Meat Company. They wanted to put their name up in lights. Banned from putting up an advert, they built the windows of the tower in shapes that just so happened to resemble an O, an X and another O.

Everybody still calls it the OXO Tower, but OXO Tower Wharf (oxotower.co.uk) is now owned and managed by a local social enterprise, the Coin Street Community Builders, and houses co-operative flats, design studios, shops, galleries, restaurants and cafés.

FOWL PLAY

In December 1945 six men staged an armed robbery at the OXO Tower, stealing more than 100 turkeys!

Channelling 'warehouse chic'

The tower is lit red at night

ALL THE PIES

In the 1970s the building was used for producing 'long eggs' for the middle of meat pies!

EXCLUSIVE EATS

The exclusive Oxo Tower Brasserie is on the building's 8th floor, with priceless views of the city. You won't find any OXO cubes on the menu here!

BATTERSEA POWER STATION

Battersea Power Station is one of South London's best-known monuments, its four smokestacks famously celebrated on Pink Floyd's *Animals* album cover. It was designed by the same person who created the city's iconic red telephone box (see pAGE 12). The station was snuffed out in 1983 and left in limbo for more than 30 years, but it's now being redeveloped as seriously fancy flats, shops and restaurants. There will be two brand new tube stations and the US Embassy is even relocating nearby.

The station's iconic white chimneys have been painstakingly dismantled, restored and reconstructed brick by brick to make them shiny and new.

The building was designed to look like a cathedral. It is Europe's largest brick building.

10 DOWNING STREET

CITY OF WESTMINSTER

Downing Street is named after the grumpy former diplomat George Downing.

Britain's prime minister (PM) has lived at Number 10 Downing Street since 1735. Here, for nearly three centuries PMs have eaten, drunk, snoozed and run the country (not necessarily all at once). Recent years have seen some PMs moving to the more spacious apartment at 11 Downing Street.

The glossy black door at Number 10 looks like painted wood but it was actually replaced with bomb-proof metal in 1991. There is a brass doorbell but no one rings it as the door is watched via security cameras 24/7. PMs are never even given the keys to their home! Armed guards let them in and out instead.

IMAGINE THE STORIES WE MOGGIES COULD TELL!

PALMERSTON

CHIEF MOUSER

Number 10 is one of the most heavily guarded buildings in Britain, and it's even protected from mice. It has its own cat – Larry – with the official title Chief Mouser. He can often be found fighting with his black-and-white rival, Palmerston, who is CM at the Foreign and Commonwealth Office. Both were originally rescue cats.

MELLOW YELLOW

10 Downing St is painted black but the bricks are actually yellow underneath. The city's smog made the originals so dirty that they had to be painted during the 1960s.

LARRY

TURN OVER TO MAKE

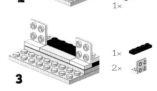

YOU CAN MAKE IT

NUMBER 10

Make your own mini replica of the most famous door in the world. It's not bomb-proof but it looks good enough for a PM.

BRICKS NEEDED

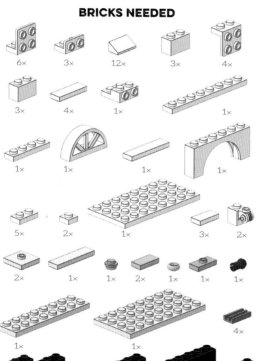

6×   3×   12×   3×   4×

3×   4×   1×   1×

1×   1×   1×   1×

5×   2×   1×   3×   2×

2×   1×   1×   2×   1×   1×   1×

1×   1×   4×

1×   2×   5×   1×   2×

2×   1×   2×   1×   2×   1×   3×   1×

1   1×   1×

2   2×   1×   1×

3   1×   2×

4   2×   1×

5   1×   2×   2×   2×

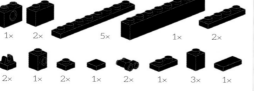

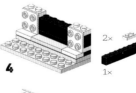

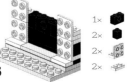

Houses of Parliament

The Houses of Parliament is the heart of UK politics. Officially called the Palace of Westminster, the oldest part is the medieval Westminster Hall. More than 900 years old, it is one of only a few bits that survived a raging fire in 1834. That was particularly lucky as the amazing 1394 roof was the first of its kind. Despite being made of huge, heavy wooden beams, it isn't held up by a single column!

CONSTITUTIONALLY, THE QUEEN IS NOT ALLOWED TO ENTER THE HOUSE OF COMMONS

WESTMINSTER BRIDGE IS PAINTED THE SAME GREEN AS THE BENCHES

Westminster Hall's unique roof

'Frontbenchers' sit and debate here

Two sides of the house

Parliament is split into two 'houses' who sit in different rooms. The green House of Commons is the lower house, where elected Members of Parliament (MPs) sit. The members of the red-decorated House of Lords traditionally inherited their titles, but nowadays it also has peers selected in other ways. Both houses debate and vote on laws, which are then presented to the Queen. At the annual State Opening of Parliament in May, the Queen takes her throne in the House of Lords, having arrived in her gold-trimmed Irish State Coach from Buckingham Palace (her crown travels alone in its very own coach). Bling, much?!

THE BIG GUY

You'll recognise the Elizabeth Tower. That's the real name for Big Ben, the world-famous clock tower at the Houses of Parliament. Big Ben is actually the biggest bell inside, which first chimed in 1859. It weighs as much as a small elephant, and when it was first made it needed 16 horses to haul it through London to the tower. Londoners soon nicknamed it, but no one is quite sure why.

Big Ben is accurate to the second

BIG BEN IN NUMBERS

2.7m- (9ft-) long hour-hand

4.2m- (14ft-) long minute-hand

7m- (23ft-) wide dials

60cm- (2ft-) high numbers

Tower of London

The Tower of London has a dark past. Its 1,000 years of history echo with the crimes and punishments of monarchs, traitors and torturers. It is a formidable royal fortress, medieval palace and priceless treasure house.

Off with their heads

There was once a time when anyone important who upset a monarch risked having their head cut off here, on Tower Green. Most prisoners had their heads lopped off in front of a baying crowd on Tower Hill, but this five-star spot was reserved for the most important aristocratic prisoners. Three English queens were beheaded here: Anne Boleyn (1536), Catherine Howard (1542) and Lady Jane Grey (1554). There is now a glass cushion memorial in the exact spot.

BEEFY SECURITY

Forty Yeoman Warders guard the Tower of London. They live with their families in the Tower and are nicknamed 'Beefeaters' because they were originally paid with meat instead of money. Their job is a ceremonial one even though they are all ex-soldiers. One Beefeater has the title of 'Ravenmaster' as he looks after the ravens.

A Beefeater in uniform

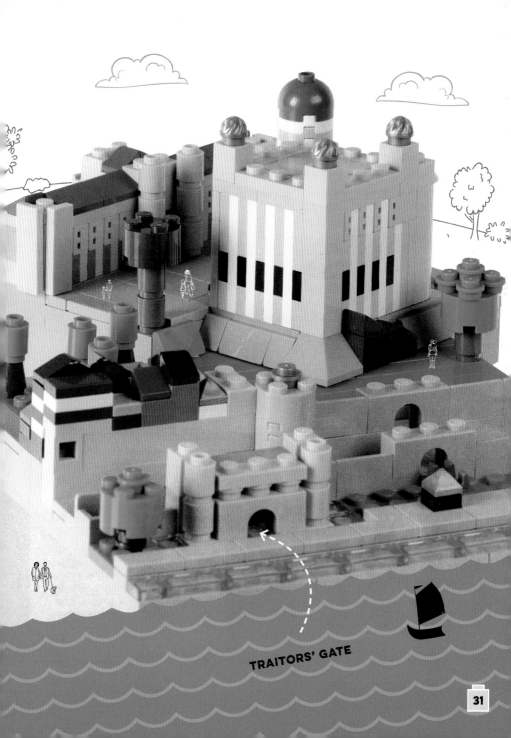

TRAITORS' GATE

Crown Jewels

Imperial Crown of India, worn by George V

The Tower of London's Waterloo Barracks is the home of the crown jewels, which are in a very real sense priceless. The royal family's most precious jewels are kept under strict lock and key. The British crown jewels include ten – yes, ten – crowns! There are also swords, orbs, sceptres and other bling things needed to crown British monarchs. The whole super-shiny collection is kept behind extra-thick glass and protected by the hi-tech security. That's because it's worth £3–5 billion ($5–8 billion)!

The tower also has an extensive armoury

IMPERIAL BLING

The Imperial State Crown is set with 2,868 diamonds, including the 317-carat Second Star of Africa (Cullinan II). The oldest stone is probably the St Edward's Sapphire. It's said to be from a ring worn by Edward the Confessor, the king nearly 1,000 years ago. Edward's grave was opened and it was taken from his finger. The crown is worn by the Queen at the State Opening of Parliament (see p.46).

THE BIG ONE

The State Sceptre with Cross is topped with the largest colourless diamond in the world – the First Star of Africa (or Cullinan I). It was cut from the biggest diamond ever found, which was more than 10cm (4in) long. Discovered in a South African mine, one of the managers poked it out of a tunnel wall with his stick.

STOP THIEF!

In 1671, Thomas Blood and his gang tried to steal the crown jewels and nearly got away with it. Blood tricked the keeper of the jewels into letting him see them. Then he knocked the keeper out, flattened Edward's crown with a mallet and hid it under his cloak. He even stuffed an orb down his breeches!

TURN OVER TO MAKE

YOU CAN MAKE IT!

Orb

The queen's orb features amethyst, diamonds, rubies, pearls, sapphires and emeralds. This model is a bit less expensive to build…!

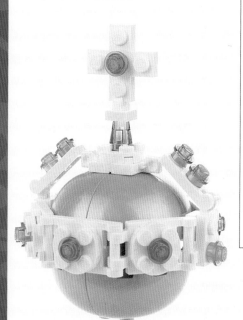

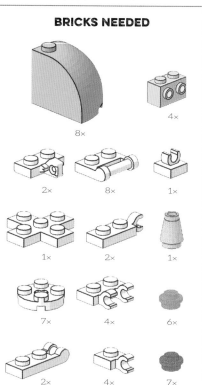

BRICKS NEEDED

8×

4×

2×

8×

1×

1×

2×

1×

7×

4×

6×

2×

4×

7×

1

4×

2

4×

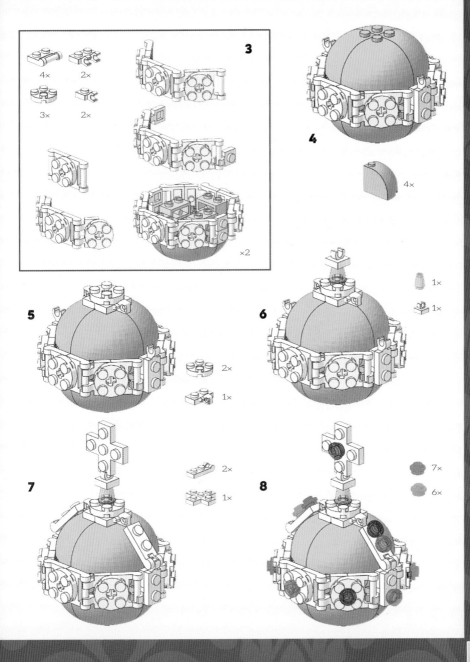

3

4× 2×

3× 2×

×2

4

4×

5

2×

1×

6

1×

1×

7

2×

1×

8

7×

6×

Raven

Ravens have lived at the Tower of London for centuries. Legend has it that if they ever leave, the kingdom will fall, so there are always at least six of them kept at the Tower by royal decree.

The birds have one wing clipped to stop them flying off but they are spoilt rotten, with daily raw meat and blood-soaked biscuits. In spite of this, birds do sometimes decide to leave, or behave so badly they have to go. One raven flew off and was last spotted outside a London pub!

YOU CAN MAKE IT!

Scientists have discovered that ravens are as intelligent as apes. This model raven certainly has a clever glint in its eye.

BRICKS NEEDED

1×   2×   2×   2×   4×   2×

1×   7×   5×   2×   4×   9×

1×   2×   2×   5×   1×   2×   3×   1×   2×   1×

5×   4×   1×   10×   2×   2×

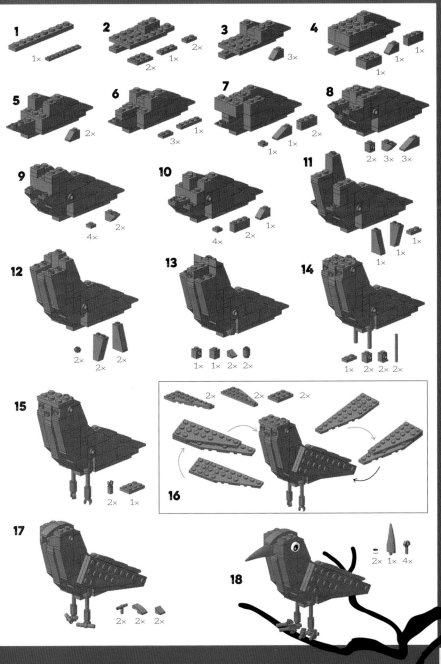

STOCKS

Life at the Tower of London was hardly a bundle of laughs. King Henry I was the first monarch to use the Royal residence as a state prison in 1100, but it was during the Tudor era in the 16th and 17th centuries that things really got nasty. Prisoners were tied on a rack and stretched, or hung by their wrists from the ceiling in manacles, to make them confess their crimes.

Royal prisoners

Hardcore criminals were not the only 'guests' – several members of the royal family were incarcerated here, too. In the 15th century, the two young sons of King Edward IV were locked up there by their uncle Richard so that he could take over the throne. In 1536 King Henry VIII had his second wife, Anne Boleyn, tried and executed here – clearing the way for him to marry someone new.

BLOODY RIVERBANKS

William the Conqueror cleverly had the Tower of London built on the banks of the River Thames – London's lifeline to and from the outside world. Prisoners sent to the Tower would arrive by boat along the river, entering through Traitors' Gate. Today, the once bloody riverbanks buzz with fun as Londoners enjoy their waterfront playground.

Horrid Henry!

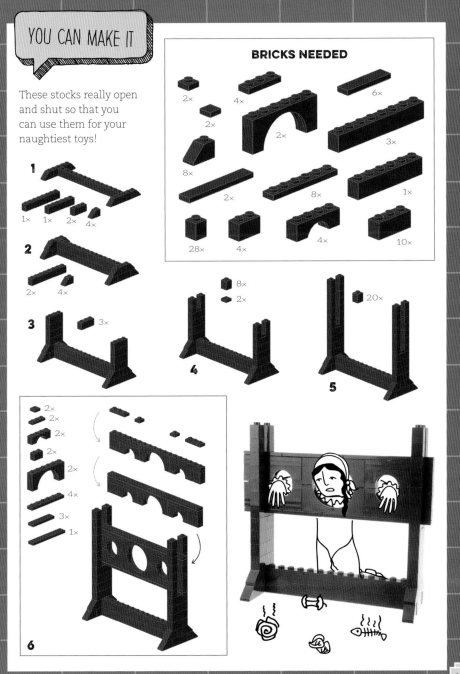

YOU CAN MAKE IT

These stocks really open and shut so that you can use them for your naughtiest toys!

BRICKS NEEDED

2× 4× 6×
2× 2×
8×
2× 3×
2× 8× 1×
28× 4× 4× 10×

1
1× 1× 2× 4×

2
2× 4×

8×
2×

3
3×

20×

4

5

6
2×
2×
2×
2×
2×
4×
3×
1×

UNION JACK

The Union Jack has been the UK's national flag since 1908. It combines England's red St George's cross, Scotland's white St Andrew's saltire and the red saltire of St Patrick to represent the island of Ireland.

When the Queen is in residence at Buckingham Place the square yellow, red and blue Royal Standard is flown; if she's not in residence, it's the Union Jack.

ZIG-A-ZIG-AH!

Geri Halliwell, aka Ginger Spice, made pop history when she performed with the Spice Girls at the 1997 BRIT Awards. She made her 'Cool Britannia' minidress by stitching a humble tea towel onto the front of a black Gucci dress. Afterwards it was later bought at auction for £41,300 ($56,856). When the Spice Girls reunited for a tour in 2007 she wore a replica covered in crystals.

Flags flying for the queen's jubilee

UK government buildings are required to fly the Union Jack at full-mast an average of 23 times a year.

Westminster Abbey

It doesn't get more royal than this. Westminster Abbey serves up the country's history on cold slabs of stone. It has been the site of the coronation of every British monarch since William the Conqueror was crowned in 1066, with the exception of a couple of unlucky Eds who were either murdered (Edward V) or retired (Edward VIII) before the magic moment.

PRINCE WILLIAM MARRIED KATE MIDDLETON HERE IN 2011.

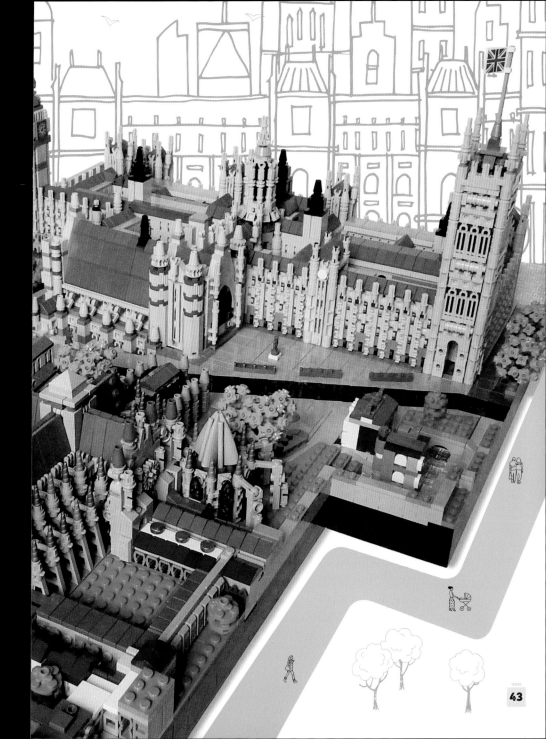

MADE FOR MONKS

When the Abbey was first built nearly 1,000 years ago it was on an island. Over time, the land has been drained so it's not on an island any more. For centuries monks lived here and the Abbey had its own farm and gardens. There's still a peaceful herb garden, where the monks once grew the plants they needed for food and to make medicine.

ST EDWARD WAS THE FOUNDER OF THE ABBEY

THE MOST SACRED SPOT IN THE ABBEY IS THE SHRINE OF ST EDWARD THE CONFESSOR

Christmas Day chaos

William the Conqueror, crowned at the Abbey on Christmas Day, 1066, had a coronation to remember. He came from Normandy in Northern France and had invaded England, forcing London to accept him as ruler. At the ceremony, the English nobles were asked to accept him as king and they shouted their agreement – which is traditional. But the French guards outside didn't know that. They thought there was trouble and started setting fire to buildings!

ST EDWARD'S REMAINS ARE THE ONLY COMPLETE SAINT'S BODY IN BRITAIN. OTHERS HAVE BEEN SPLIT APART TO BE USED AS HOLY RELICS

YUCK!

THE END IS NIGH

In front of the Abbey's altar a marble pavement from 1268 predicts the end of the world in AD 19,693, so we have a little way to go still!

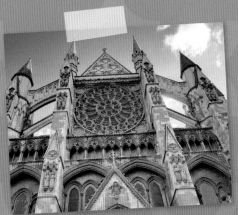

The Abbey's grand north entrance

THE ORIGINAL BUILDING WAS DECLARED HOLY JUST A FEW WEEKS BEFORE ST EDWARD'S DEATH

ROYAL RESTING PLACE

Among the 450 tombs and monuments are 17 monarch's graves, including those of Tudor rulers Henry VIII, Mary and Elizabeth I. It's also the final resting place of many notable non-royals, including scientists Charles Darwin and Sir Isaac Newton, authors Geoffrey Chaucer and Charles Dickens, and many other greats (William Shakespeare, Jane Austen, Charlotte Brontë).

Coronation Chair

The wooden Coronation Chair at Westminster Abbey was made on the orders of Edward I in 1300. He had a space put underneath to house the Stone of Scone – the sacred stone of Scotland that Scottish kings sit on when they get crowned. Now the stone is in Edinburgh Castle but it will be brought back for future coronations. Every monarch since the early 14th century has been crowned on this chair (apart from joint-monarchs Mary II and William III, who had their own chairs fashioned for the event).

SPLINTERED BUT SURVIVED

In 1914, suffragettes fighting for women's votes put a small bomb underneath, which blew a piece off. Then in 1950, Scottish students stole the Stone of Scone from under it, damaging the chair and accidentally dropping the stone and breaking it in half.

SCHOOLBOY GRAFFITI

The Coronation Chair had lots of graffiti carved on it by Westminster schoolboys in the 1700s and 1800s.

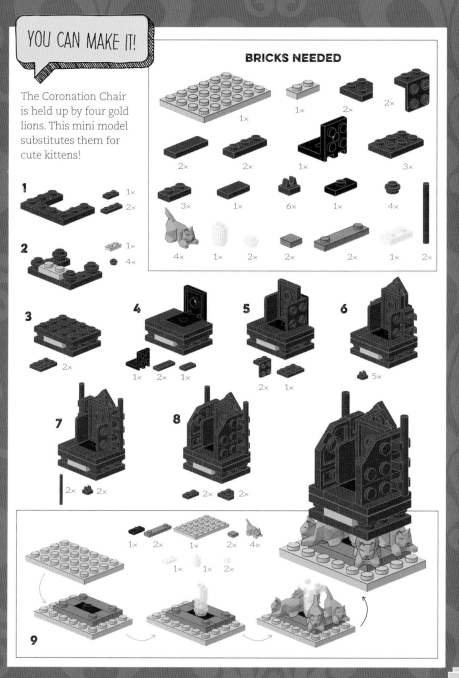

YOU CAN MAKE IT!

The Coronation Chair is held up by four gold lions. This mini model substitutes them for cute kittens!

BRICKS NEEDED

TRAFALGAR SQUARE

Trafalgar Square is the true centre of London, where thousands of revellers see in the New Year, and locals congregate for open-air cinema, Christmas celebrations and political protests. It is dominated by the 52m- (170ft-) high Nelson's Column, which honours Admiral Lord Horatio Nelson, who led his fleet's heroic victory over Napoleon in 1805. It is ringed by four large bronze lions.

'The Invisible Enemy Should Not Exist'

The Fourth Plinth

Three of the square's four plinths are occupied by nobles. The fourth plinth remained empty for more than 150 years until the Royal Society of Arts used it to create the Fourth Plinth Commission, 'the smallest sculpture park in the world'. Changing artworks include a clear resin copy of the plinth turned upside down, a giant thumbs-up, a bright blue cockerel and a winged bull made from tin cans, see above.

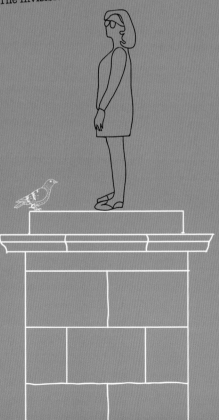

**THE WORLDS
SMALLEST
SCULPTURE
PARK**

AS PART OF AN ADVERTISING STUNT, SPEAKERS WERE HIDDEN BEHIND THE LIONS SO THAT PASSERS-BY WOULD THINK THEY WERE COMING TO LIFE!

ROAR!

Bronze won in battle

The bronze used to make the lions came from cannons captured from the Battle of Trafalgar – Nelson's greatest victory. His forces beat Napoleon in a sea battle but he paid with his life when he was shot on deck by a French sniper. His statue stands on top of the column, minus an eye and an arm, both which he lost whilst fighting.

Nelson at the Battle of Trafalgar

CAT PAWS

Victorian artist Sir Edwin Landseer was commissioned to design grander lions but it took him nine years to create them. He visited London Zoo to watch the lions there and asked if he could have a dead one. It took years for a lion to die but eventually he got one. He started to make models of it, but the body began to rot before he could finish, which is why the lions have pet cat paws.

Nelson's column in Trafalgar Square

THE LIONS IN NUMBERS

3.4m (11ft) high
6.1m (20ft) long
27 parts are riveted together per lion

CITY OF LONDON
DRAGON

The City of London's official symbol is the dragon – and that's why there are so many of these magical beasts infesting the capital! The boundaries marking the edges of the city are guarded by silver dragons standing on plinths, with upswept wings and pointed tongues, holding shields and swords. The original inspiration was the two 2.1m- (7ft-) high dragons on Victoria Embankment.

BEASTS OF THE BOROUGH

Each London borough has its own coat-of-arms and many of them show mythical (and real) beasts, including lions, griffins, dragons, stags, boars and bulls.

GGGGRRR!

SCALY SLEEPOVERS

London's Natural History Museum is home to reconstructed skeletons of the original mega-monsters – dinosaurs! Life-size animatronic dinos roar at visitors as they walk past, including a terrifying moving T. rex that senses passers-by and bares its teeth! The bravest enthusiasts can book in for a sleepover at the museum or a torch-lit tour of the dino gallery.

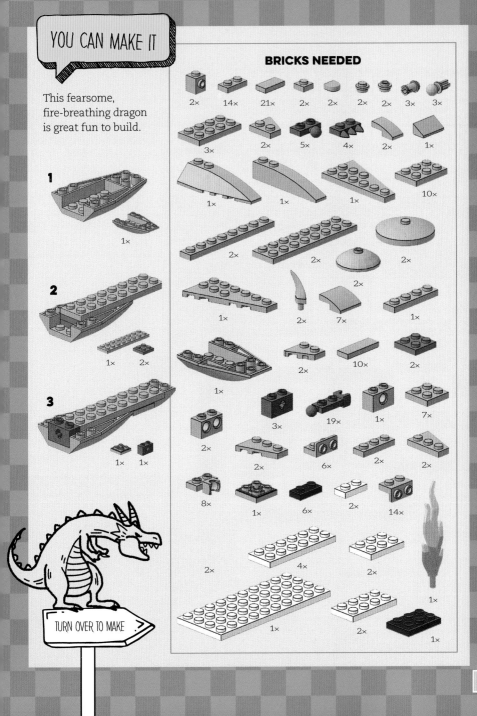

YOU CAN MAKE IT

This fearsome, fire-breathing dragon is great fun to build.

BRICKS NEEDED

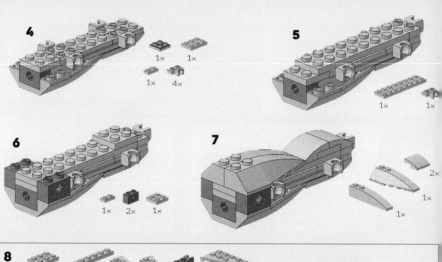

4

1× 1×

1× 4×

5

1× 1×

6

1× 2× 1×

7

2×

1×

1×

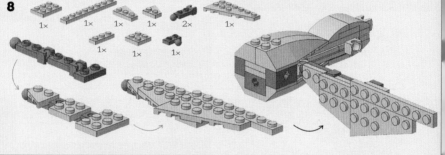

8

1× 1× 1× 1× 2× 1×

1× 1×

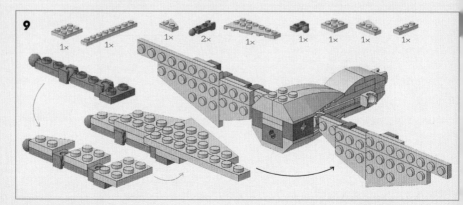

9

1× 1×

1× 2× 1× 1× 1× 1× 1×

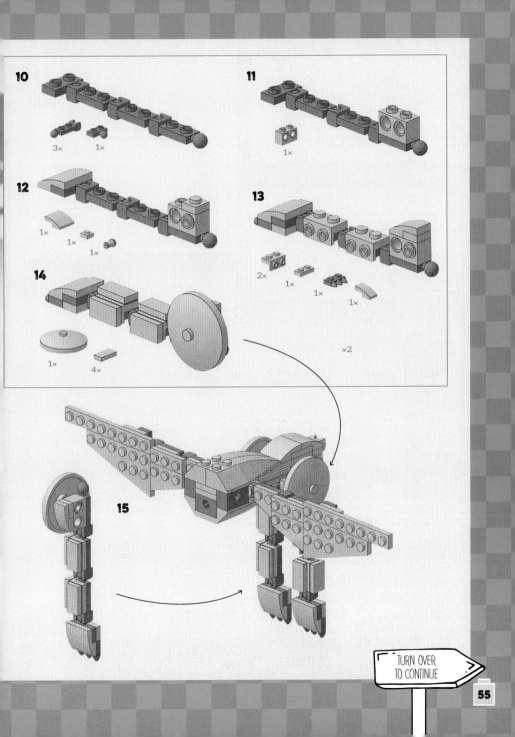

10

3× 1×

11

1×

12

1× 1× 1×

13

2× 1× 1× 1×

14

1× 4×

×2

15

TURN OVER TO CONTINUE

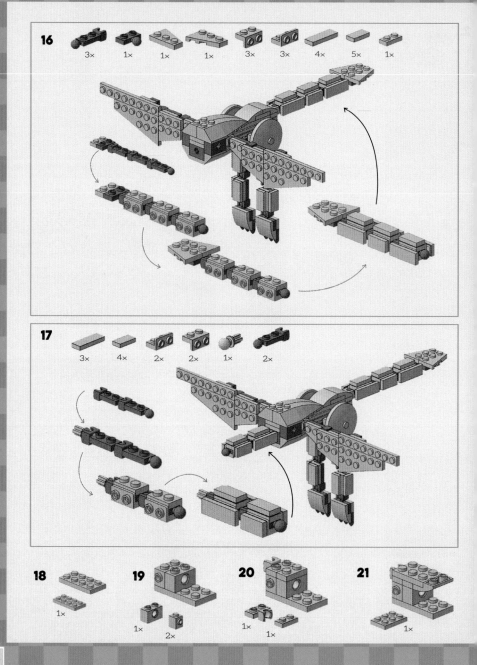

16

3× 1× 1× 1× 3× 3× 4× 5× 1×

17

3× 4× 2× 2× 1× 2×

18 1×

19 1× 2×

20 1× 1×

21 1×

22 1× 1× 1×

23 1× 1× 1× 2×

24 1× 2× 2×

25 1× 2× 2×

26

27 2× 1× 2× 2× 1× 2× 1× 1×

2×

28 1×

29 2× 2×

30 2× 2×

31 2×

32 1× 4×

33 2× 1× 6× 2×

34 2× 1× 6× 1×

The London Eye

The London Eye is the world's biggest rotating observation wheel, 135m (443ft) tall and 120m (394ft) wide. On a clear day the views stretch 40km (25 miles) – that's about as far as Windsor Castle so remember to wave at the queen. More than 3.5 million people cram into its 32 capsules every year. That's more than visit the Egyptian pyramids or India's Taj Mahal!

The Eye overlooks the River Thames. England's longest river runs right through the city and it was probably the reason why people settled here in the first place, around 750,000 years ago when it was a marshy wilderness. The first Londoners built their prehistoric huts where they could fish and get across the river. They built wooden walkways over the marshes, too. The remains of one walkway were discovered in Greenwich, dating back 6,000 years. That's more than 500 years older than Stonehenge!

MUDDY LARKS

Muddying your hands might sound like a laugh but imagine having to do it to stay alive. 'Mudlarks' were poor Victorian children who scrabbled on the river's banks looking for things to sell. They savenged wood, tin or, if they were lucky, a lost brooch.

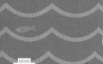

CLEOPATRA'S NEEDLE

No single monument captures the English love of history and eccentricity quite like Cleopatra's Needle. The Egyptian obelisk was transported to London in 1877 and planted on the Victoria Embankment a year later. A time capsule was hidden in its base. Its said to include a portrait of Queen Victoria, a railway guide, hairpins, the *Bible*, toys, a baby's bottle and pictures of English beauties of the day.

Sphinxes guard the needle's base

Large parts of London are below the high-water mark of the River Thames. The Embankment was built between 1864 and 1870 and is an amazing feat of engineering that channels the water between its huge walls. It stops large areas of the city from being flooded. It also provided places for boats to dock and for pedestrians to walk.

The needle is around 3,460 years old and comes from an ancient city called Heliopolis. The hieroglyphs all over it commemorate Ancient Egyptian battle victories and are actually nothing to do with Cleopatra. It was given to Britain in the 1800s by the ruler of Egypt and was sailed over to the UK. During the voyage a storm killed six crewmen and the needle was nearly lost for good, leading people to say it was cursed.

Queen's Guards

The Queen of England lives at Buckingham Palace. The grand white building is used to host state visits, royal ceremonies and Her Majesty's famous garden parties. Queen Elizabeth II divides her time between here, Windsor Castle and Balmoral castle in Scotland.

The Queen's Guards stand on duty at Buckingham Palace and St James's Palace. They sport red tunics and bearskin hats in summer and greatcoats in winter. Their uniforms come from a time when soldiers fought on foot. The tall bearskin caps were devised to make them look taller in battle and their red tunics made it harder for the enemy to count them on the battlefield (they tend to blur into each other in a crowd).

BUCKINGHAM PALACE IN NUMBERS

78 bathrooms

350 clocks

775 rooms

EAT LIKE A ROYAL

Buckingham Palace is also the venue for royal banquets. It takes three days to lay the enormous table with thousands of pieces of cutlery, glasses and napkins. Each guest gets a space of 42cm (16.5in) for their setting, and it's all carefully measured. During the mega-dinners there are so many courses that staff use a traffic-light system behind the scenes.

THE WORLD'S MOST EXPENSIVE HOME

The London home of the queen is officially the world's most expensive, worth over £1 billion ($1.4 billion). Its Throne Room boasts two pink velvet chairs with golden sphinx-shaped armrests and his-and-hers monograms. For Prince William's wedding it became a 'chillax' room, complete with DJ.

TURN OVER TO MAKE >

Queen's Guards

The guards at Buckingham Palace
are strictly forbidden from smiling.
This model is similarly stony-faced.

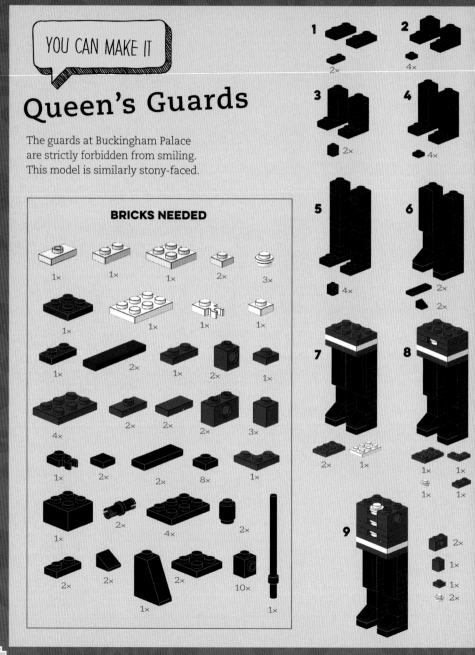

BRICKS NEEDED

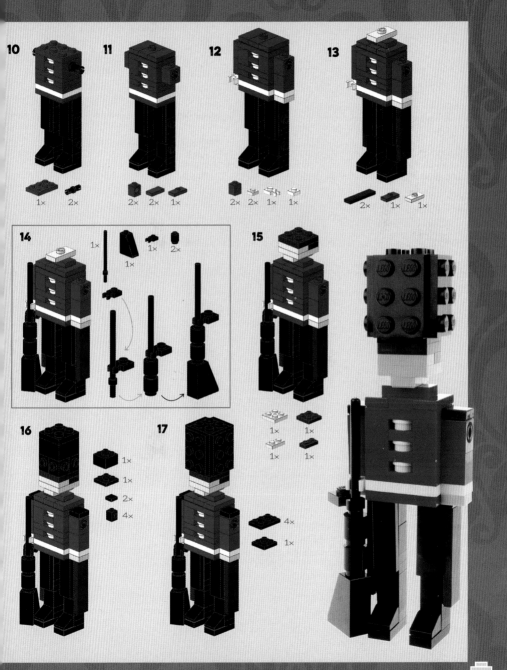

ST PAUL'S CATHEDRAL

THE BIGGEST BELLS ARE GREAT PAUL, WEIGHING MORE THAN A MALE ELEPHANT, AND GREAT TOM, WEIGHING AS MUCH AS A FEMALE ELEPHANT

Royal events aplenty have taken place at St Paul's Cathedral, including luxurious weddings. It was designed by Sir Christopher Wren, who wanted to make a dome that was grand on the outside but not too echoey and large on the inside. The solution was to build it in three layers, like the inside of an onion. This unique structure made the cathedral Wren's masterpiece.

ST PAUL'S BOASTS 12 BELLS AND ONE OF THE LOUDEST PEALS IN THE WORLD.

View from the Whispering Gallery

GREAT TOM

GREAT TOM TOLLS OUT THE BAD NEWS IF A MEMBER OF THE ROYAL FAMILY DIES.

BT Tower

Owned by phone company BT, the BT Tower was the city's tallest structure when it opened in 1966 and visible from almost everywhere in central London. Strangely, the tower was an official 'secret' and didn't appear on maps until 1993, when Member of Parliament Kate Hoey used her parliamentary privilege to 'confirm' its existence!

The tower is still a major communications hub and doubles up as an air-pollution monitor. It is also a listed building, which means getting special permission to change it.

50TH BIRTHDAY

To mark the tower's 50th anniversary, its revolving restaurant reopened its doors for two weeks only. The Top of the Tower restaurant was an icon. In the 1960s Muhammad Ali, Tom Jones and The Beatles were among the 4,000 daily visitors.

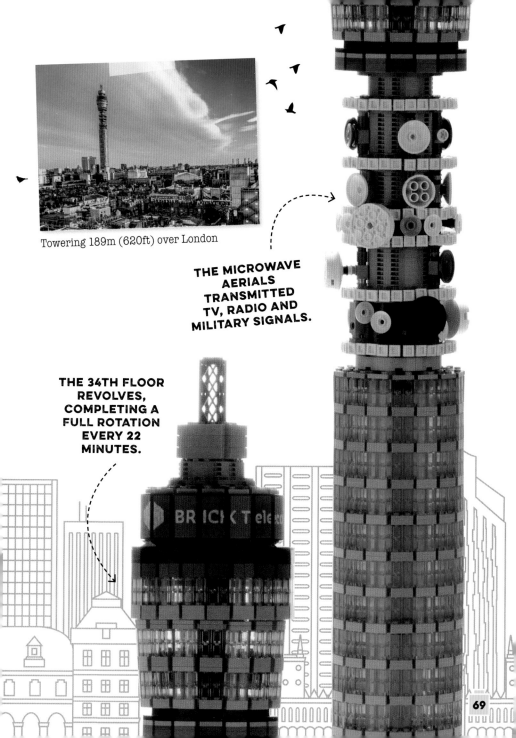

Towering 189m (620ft) over London

THE MICROWAVE AERIALS TRANSMITTED TV, RADIO AND MILITARY SIGNALS.

THE 34TH FLOOR REVOLVES, COMPLETING A FULL ROTATION EVERY 22 MINUTES.

BR ICK T ele

69

THE BRITISH MUSEUM

The country's largest museum and one of the oldest and finest in the world, this famous museum is home to Egyptian, Etruscan, Greek, Roman, European and Middle Eastern treasures, among others. Inside, the Great Court has an amazing glass-and-steel latticed roof. At its centre is the Reading Room – Mahatma Gandhi was a cardholder.

Some of the most interesting artefacts here are: the Rosetta Stone, the key to deciphering Egyptian hieroglyphics; the controversial Parthenon Sculptures, taken from Athens by Lord Elgin; the collection of Egyptian mummies.

BURIED TREASURE

460 years ago someone was on the run and had to bury a fortune fast! That's thought to be the story behind the Fishpool Hoard – 1,237 gold coins (plus jewellery) now on display. It was a time of rebellion and the person who buried the stash could have been on the losing side of a battle.

The Great Court and latticed roof

The Fishpool Hoard was worth £300,000 ($459,570) when it was buried.

TURN OVER TO MAKE

THE BRITISH MUSEUM

The museum entrance has sculptures that show the human race being educated by its artefacts. This model will certainly give you a fun lesson in LEGO® building!

BRICKS NEEDED

4×
10×
5×
1×
4×
4×
6×
3×

4×
22×
9×
20×

4×
4×
6×
42×
8×

2×
3×
2×
4×
16×

12×
14×

2×
4×
2×
25×
6×

19×
30×
19×
3×
16×

15×
16×
16×

1

4×

5

6×   4×   25×   6×   8×   2×

9

16×   16×

13

2×   2×   19×   3×   19×

17

10×   1×   1×   4×

2

2× 6× 20×

3

2× 20×

4

5× 1× 3×

6

2× 16× 28×

7

2× 7× 7× 8×

8

8× 12×

10

2× 1×

11

22× 4× 2× 2×

12

4× 2× 3×

14

2× 2× 2× 2×

15

1× 1× 2× 1× 4×

16

2× 1× 3× 4× 10×

18

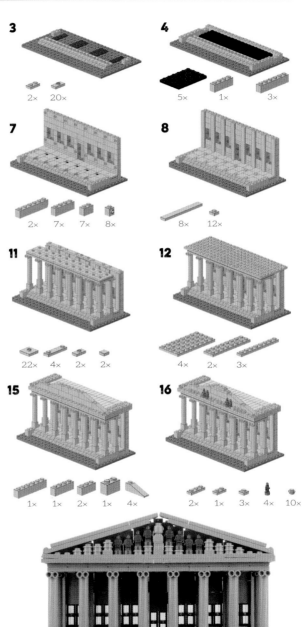

The Shard

Only Londoners can dine in a glass Shard, work inside a Cheese Grater, shop in a Stealth Bomber and negotiate business deals in a Gherkin. These are the names of some of 21st-century-London's newest buildings. The Walkie Talkie is a skyscraper shaped like a hand-held radio. This feat of engineering quickly earned the nickname 'Walkie Scorchie' after cars parked beneath its reflective exterior started melting in the sun!

There are a total of 82 floors in the skyscraper

FEARLESS FOX

When The Shard was being built a wild fox
managed to get in and climb up to the
72nd floor, where he lived eating food
scraps left lying around by the builders.
When he was discovered staff nicknamed
him Romeo. He was rescued, checked
by vets and then set free, back to
his life roaming the streets.

The Shard is the highest skyscraper
in Western Europe (310m/1,017ft). It
has 95 storeys, which pack in award-
winning restaurants, a five-star hotel,
offices and London's highest viewing
gallery. The architect, Renzo Piano,
wanted the building to look like an
iceberg rising from the river nearby.

LONDON MONUMENT

In 1666, the Great Fire of London started in a bakery in Pudding Lane and soon swept through the whole city, destroying thousands of homes. Much of the medieval city was destroyed, with 13,200 houses reduced to rubble and an estimated 70,000 people made homeless (though only a half-dozen died).

The fire is commemorated by the Monument – the world's tallest individual stone column, designed by Sir Christopher Wren. Its height is the exact distance from the column to the place where the fire began, and the gleaming golden urn on top symbolises flames.

Urn on the monument's top

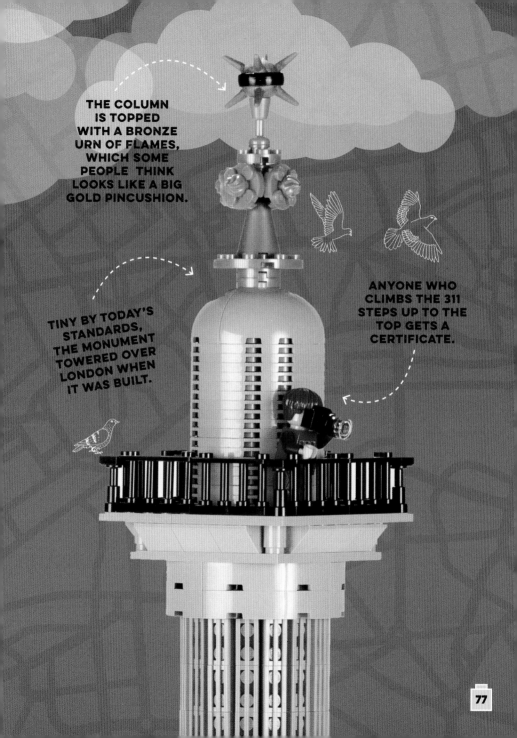

THE COLUMN IS TOPPED WITH A BRONZE URN OF FLAMES, WHICH SOME PEOPLE THINK LOOKS LIKE A BIG GOLD PINCUSHION.

TINY BY TODAY'S STANDARDS, THE MONUMENT TOWERED OVER LONDON WHEN IT WAS BUILT.

ANYONE WHO CLIMBS THE 311 STEPS UP TO THE TOP GETS A CERTIFICATE.

Fish and Chips

Nothing else says 'England' quite like the smell of frying fish! Fish and chips often tops the list of the nation's favourite food (occasionally falling behind chicken tikka masala). It's traditionally served wrapped in old newspaper and sprinkled generously with salt and malt vinegar. It's usually made with Atlantic cod, but 'chippies' are starting to fry a wider range of fish to conserve the ocean's stocks. Weird and wonderful side dishes include mushy peas and pickled eggs!

A SLIPPERY MEAL

Jellied eels are London's original fast food. Fished for in the River Thames, the wriggling delicacy was cooked, left to cool and only eaten when the liquid had turned to jelly – slime heaven!

THE FIRST CHIP SHOP IN THE WORLD WAS OPENED IN OLD FORD ROAD, EAST LONDON, IN 1860 BY JOSEPH MALIN.

YOU CAN MAKE IT!

These models look good enough to eat – complete with chips and mushy peas, or an accompaniment of your choice!

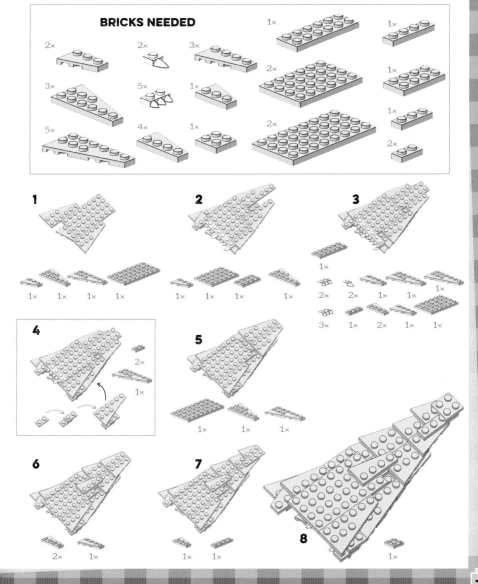

BRICKS NEEDED

2× 2× 3× 1× 1×

3× 5× 1× 2× 1×

5× 4× 1× 2× 1×

2×

1

1× 1× 1× 1×

2

1× 1× 1× 1×

3

1×

2× 2× 1× 1× 1×

3× 1× 2× 1× 1×

4

2×

1×

5

1× 1× 1×

6

2× 1×

7

1× 1×

8

1×

BOROUGH MARKET

Located in the same spot since the 13th century, 'London's Larder' has experienced an amazing rebirth in the past 15 years. Borough Market is always overflowing with food lovers, gastronomes, wide-eyed visitors and Londoners in search of inspiration for their dinner party. The market specialises in upmarket fresh produce. There are plenty of takeaway stands and an almost unreasonable number of cake stalls. Yum!

PRIZED PARMESAN

London diarist Samuel Pepys was caught in the Great Fire of London in 1666 and had to save his most valuable possessions – including a giant wheel of Parmesan cheese! It was too heavy to carry, so he buried it in his garden. Parmesan was very costly in his day. Even today, valuable Parmesans are sometimes stored in bank vaults.

Borough Market today

TRAFFIC CHAOS

In the 1700s the market was a much less orderly affair with stalls spilling out all over Borough High Street and causing traffic mayhem. There was an Act of Parliament to close down the market in the streets, which is when it moved to its current location.

FOOD TRUCK

TOP OF THE TRUCKS

The UK chain MEATliquor started life as a burger van in 2009. Now with 11 restaurants, it made a profit of £17million ($22.5 million) in 2016.

Food is big business in London. The city's colourful markets and vacant street corners are increasingly occupied by independent food trucks, many of them in repurposed vintage vehicles such as horse boxes, school buses and even Airstream caravans. On sale are freshly cooked bites from around the globe, from steaming pork buns to bulging burritos and deep-fried churros dipped in chocolate sauce. Yum!

The KERB collective is the heart of London's street food revolution, attracting the very best food on wheels to sites around the city. Vendors call themselves 'KERB-anists'. Pistachio-butter doughnuts anyone?

TURN OVER TO MAKE

YOU CAN MAKE IT!

Make your very easy-to-build food truck. Hipster staff not included!

BRICKS NEEDED

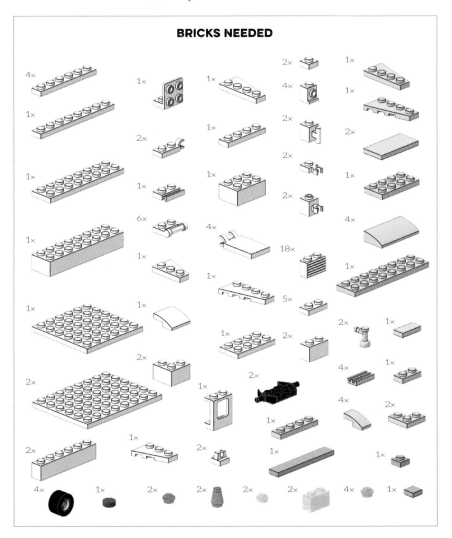

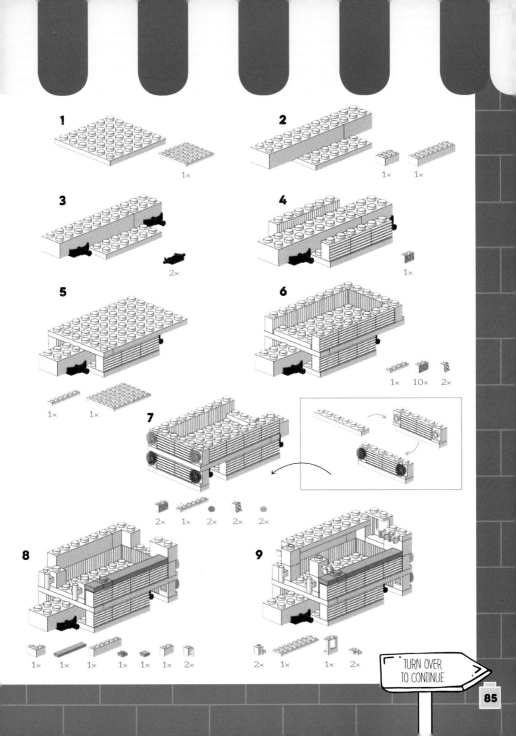

1

1×

2

1× 1×

3

2×

4

1×

5

1× 1×

6

1× 10× 2×

7

2× 1× 2× 2× 2×

8

1× 1× 1× 1× 1× 1× 2×

9

2× 1× 1× 2×

TURN OVER TO CONTINUE

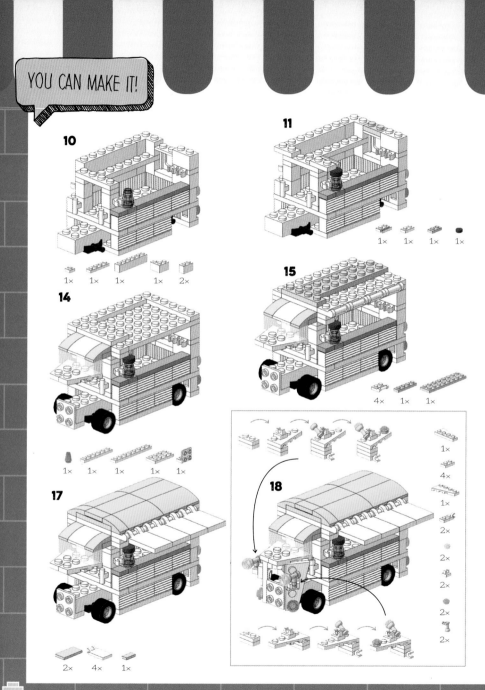

YOU CAN MAKE IT!

86

12

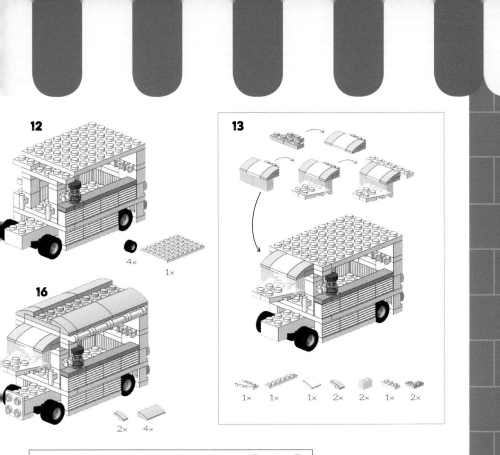

4× 1×

13

16

2× 4×

1× 1× 1× 2× 2× 1× 2×

19

4× 1× 1×

1× 2×

Afternoon Tea

Fortnum & Mason is one of London's poshest grocers. It has sold tea for 300 years, and the tea salon there is a top spot to sip a brew and nibble cucumber sandwiches and jam-slathered scones.

The habit of having afternoon tea and cakes caught on in London in the 1800s. It became a grand party event, with people sending invitations to their friends and wearing their best gloves to eat their cakes and sandwiches.

THE BEES' KNEES

Four beautiful gilded beehives are kept on the roof of Fortnum and Mason. The bees make top quality honey for the shop's customers.

CUPPA ROSIE LEE

Only Londoners born within hearing distance of the bells of St Mary-Le-Bow Church are true 'cockneys'. East End cockneys even have their own language.

A 'CUPPA ROSIE LEE' IS A NICE CUP OF STRONG ENGLISH TEA (ALWAYS WITH MILK).

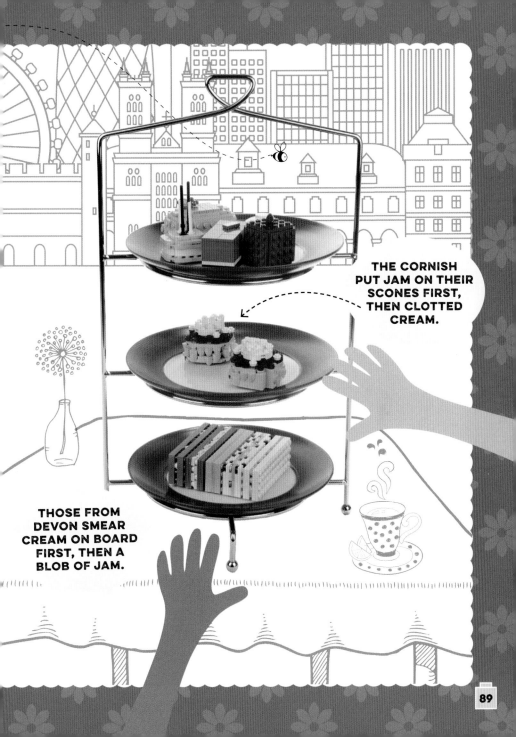

THE CORNISH PUT JAM ON THEIR SCONES FIRST, THEN CLOTTED CREAM.

THOSE FROM DEVON SMEAR CREAM ON BOARD FIRST, THEN A BLOB OF JAM.

Chinatown

Chinatown is the hub of the Chinese community in London, and when Chinese New Year comes along people in dragon and lion costumes dance through the streets here.

THEY HAVE STAG HORNS, FISH SCALES AND TIGER PAWS AND ARE SAID TO BRING GOOD LUCK.

CHINESE DRAGONS ARE NOT LIKE SCARY FIRE-BREATHING EUROPEAN DRAGONS.

London's original Chinatown was at Limehouse in the East End of London – even Sherlock Holmes shopped there.

ELEMENTARY MY DEAR...

Although it's just two streets really – this is a lively area with giant Oriental gates, Chinese street signs, pretty red lanterns, restaurants selling steaming noodles and Asian supermarkets full of curiosities. You can hear lots of different languages and dialects being spoken here, from Cantonese to Mandarin.

THE LONGER THE DRAGON, THE MORE LUCK IT BRINGS.

TURN OVER TO MAKE

Chinese Dragon

This beautiful Chinese dragon is surprisingly
easy to make as a lot of the steps are repeated.

BRICKS NEEDED

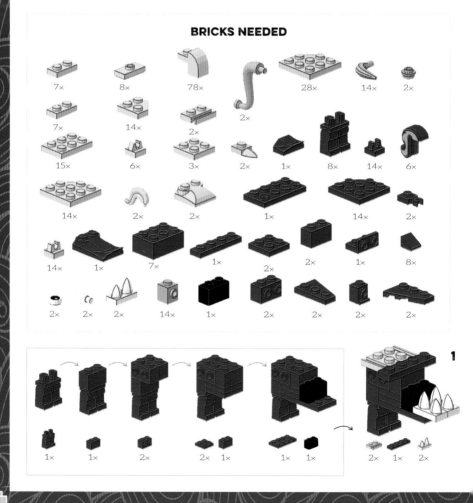

7× 8× 78× 28× 14× 2×

7× 14× 2×

15× 6× 3× 2× 1× 8× 14× 6×

14× 2× 2× 1× 14× 2×

14× 1× 7× 1× 2× 2× 1× 8×

2× 2× 2× 14× 1× 2× 2× 2× 2×

1

1× 1× 2× 2× 1× 1× 1× 2× 1× 2×

2

3

4

1× 1× 1×

2× 2× 2×

2× 2×

2× 2×

1× 1× 1× 1× 1× 3× 3×

1× 1× 1× 1× 1× 3× 3×

TURN OVER
TO CONTINUE

5

6

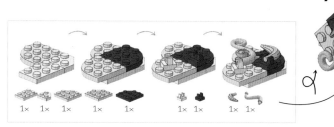

7

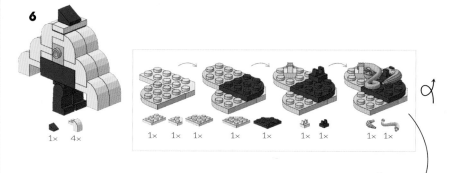

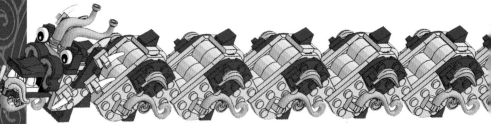

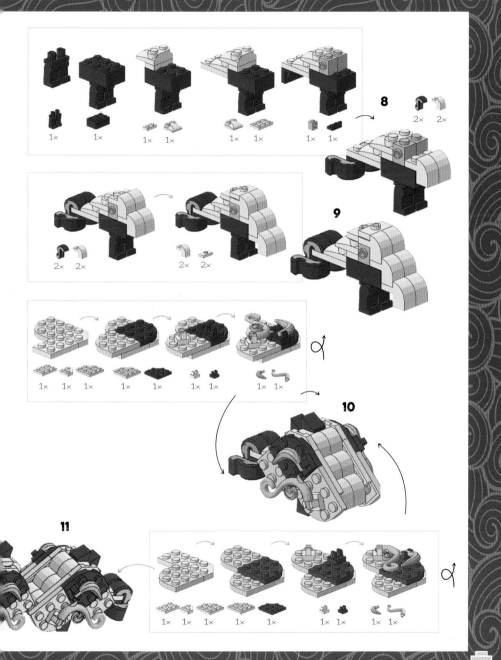

Covent Garden

Covent Garden was originally pastureland that belonged to a convent (Covent/convent – get it?), but it has had many different reincarnations. For a long while this elegant piazza hosted a bustling fruit and vegetable market.

London society gathered here in the evenings, looking for some action among the coffee houses, theatres and gambling dens. Crime was common, leading to the formation of a volunteer police force. The market still draws crowds looking for a good time and is full of street performers – from opera singers to human statues and magicians.

Inside the old market

Leicester Square to Covent Garden is London's shortest Tube journey – in fact it only takes 45 seconds!

Covent Garden is home to London's oldest restaurant – Rules on Maiden Lane. It was first opened in 1798 and serves traditional food such as game pie and oysters.

UNDERGROUND TRAIN

The London Underground – or 'Tube' – is made up of 11 colour-coded lines. Some stations, most famously Embankment and Charing Cross, are much closer in reality than they appear on the map, so you might be better off walking! Author Mark Mason walked the entire length of the London Underground – but overground – for his book *Walk the Lines*.

THE UNDERGROUND IN NUMBERS

1.03 billion passengers per year

402km (250 miles) of track

58m (190ft) down in the deepest station (Hampstead)

TRAVELLING IN STYLE

Sedan chairs were used to get around 18th-century-London. They were carried by two strong men (notorious for their terrible swearing). Inside was enough room to squeeze in the passengers' fancy wigs and gowns.

LONDON TRANSPORT MUSEUM

All aboard for a trip through London's 'wheely' interesting history. Visitors get to sit in the cab of a red bus and even drive a Tube train on a Northern Line Underground simulator.

TURN OVER TO MAKE

UNDERGROUND TRAIN

This model sports the Underground's signature go-fast white, blue and red design. Trains on the Metropolitan Line can run at up to 97km/h (60mph).

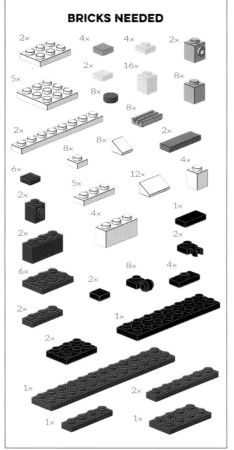

BRICKS NEEDED

2× 4× 4× 2×
5× 2× 16× 8×
8×
8×
2× 8× 2×
6× 8×
2× 5× 4× 12× 1×
2× 4× 2×
6× 8× 4×
2× 2×
2× 1×
1× 2×
1× 1×

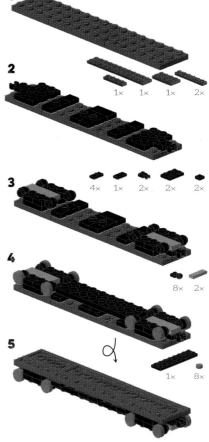

1

2 1× 1× 1× 2×

3 4× 1× 2× 2× 2×

4 8× 2×

5 1× 8×

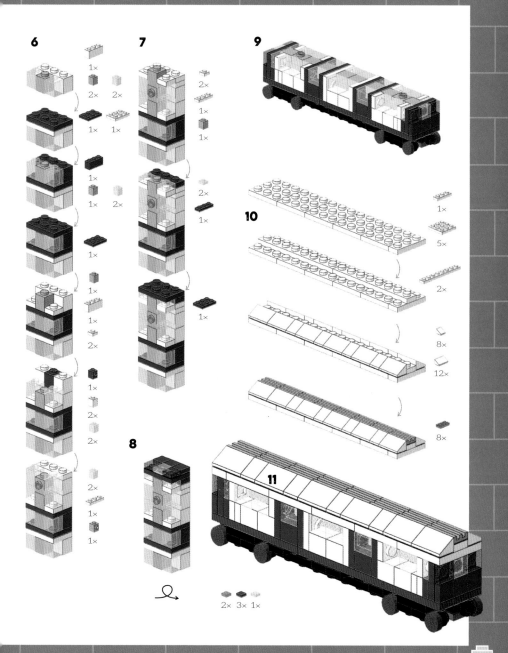

Red Buses

Everyone knows about London's famous red buses. These iconic vehicles zip around the capital at all hours of the day and night, carrying Londoners from A to B.

Six and a half million people use the city's buses every single day. The most iconic bus is the double-decker, rear-doored Routemaster. It was replaced in 2005 by more modern versions, but there are quite a few still on display and running on popular tourist routes and making everyone feel nostalgic. Ahhh.

An old-fashioned Routemaster

ALL ABOARD THE GHOST BUS

A phantom number 7 ghost bus is said to appear in the middle of the night in Cambridge Gardens, with no driver and no lights. Spooky!

ROCKING IT IN RED

Before 1907, there were lots of different coloured buses run by different companies. The London General Omnibus Company painted theirs red to stand out and they soon became the biggest bus operator in town.

ARE YOU FOR WHEEL?

Daredevil motorcycle stunt riders love to jump over London double-decker buses. Stunt star Eddie Kidd once jumped over 14!

TURN OVER TO MAKE

This bus build is cute as a button. All together now, 'the wheels on the bus go round and round…'.

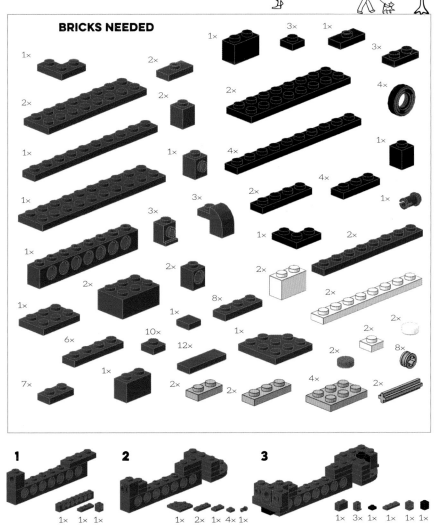

BRICKS NEEDED

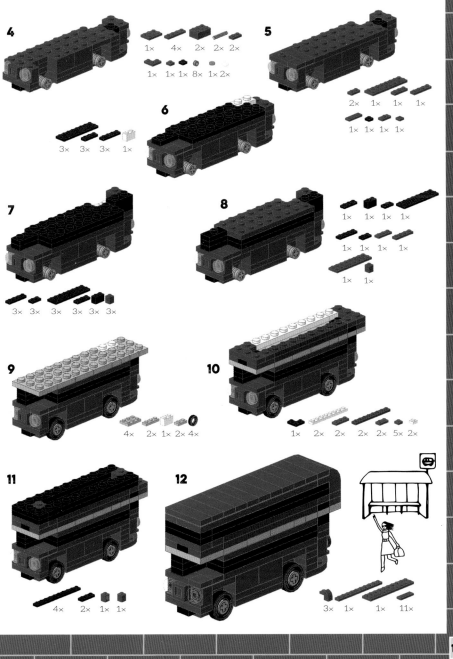

ABBEY ROAD

There are at least 10 Abbey Roads across London.

Cameras at the ready! Visitors from across the globe stride across the Abbey Road zebra crossing all day long while their friends take photos – and all because of a world-famous supergroup. The Beatles posed here for the cover of their bestselling *Abbey Road* album, released in 1969.

The Beatles crossing Abbey Road

GEORGE

PAUL

RINGO

JOHN

RAT

YOU CAN MAKE IT!

Did you know that the flashing orange lights at either end of a zebra crossing are called 'Belisha Beacons'? Us neither!

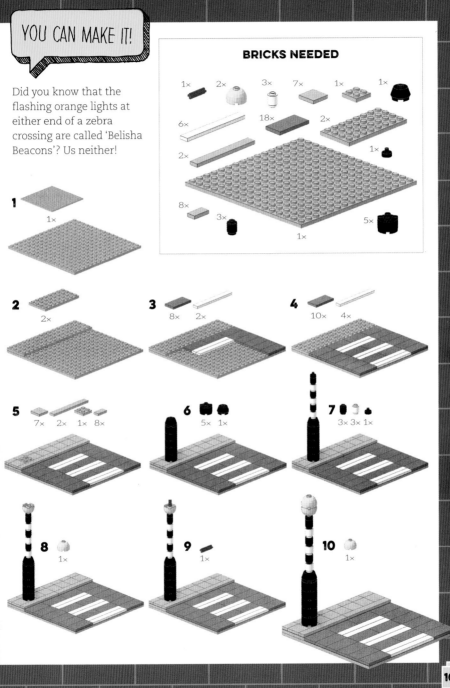

BRICKS NEEDED

107

THE ORBIT

London is the only world city to host the Olympics three times – in 1908, 1948 and 2012. Nine hundred million people worldwide tuned into the 2012 opening ceremony in East London's Olympic Park. The Orbit sculpture was designed by famous architect Sir Anish Kapoor to mark the celebrations.

GOING FOR GOLD

Among the many Olympic records broken in 2012 the most celebrated was sprinter Usain Bolt's 9.63-second 100m marvel. Things were different in the first two London Olympics. The 1908 competition included tug-of-war, powerboat racing and polo. The 1948 event included artistic events as well as sporting ones.

Bolt crossing the finishing line

Ride the slide

The twisting, turning steel structure is held together by 35,000 bolts. Brave visitors can ride the hair-raising slide from the top – it was designed by artist Carsten Höller.

CORKSCREWS TO SOLID GROUND IN JUST 40 SECONDS.

THE WORLD'S LONGEST AND TALLEST SLIDE

THRILL SEEKERS CAN ABSEIL OFF THE ORBIT!

The Orbit was sponsored by ArcelorMittal, the world's largest steel company. It is made from recycled steel.

Lord's Cricket Ground

Lord's Cricket Ground is England's 'home of cricket'. The country's most important Test matches take place here and cricket buffs (often in fancy dress!) join them for long lazy days listening to the sound of leather on willow.

ASHES TO ASHES

When the England cricket team first lost on home soil to Australia in 1882, a newspaper announced the death of English cricket. When the English team next went to Australia they were given a tiny urn representing 'the Ashes', and the two teams still play a hotly contested series of games for the Ashes to this day. The Ashes urn is sacred to cricket fans and is kept at Lord's permanently now.

YOU CAN MAKE IT!

Dibbly-dobbly, dolly catch and donkey drop…these are just a few quirky cricket terms! Luckily you don't have to be able to speak cricket to make this model.

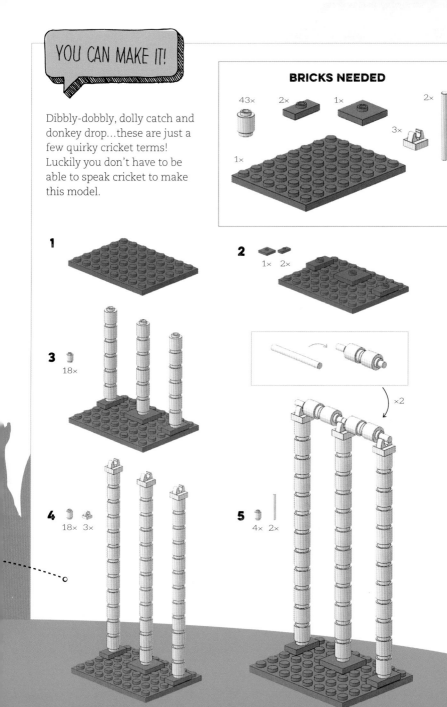

BRICKS NEEDED

43×   2×   1×   2×

3×

1×

1

2   1×   2×

3   18×

×2

4   18×   3×

5   4×   2×

Wimbledon

London may be a built-up city, but it's got plenty of room for sport. One of the top tennis competitions on the planet is played right here in the leafy suburb of Wimbledon. Nowadays it's watched by around 1.2 billion TV viewers, but the event began way back in 1877, long before TV, making it the world's oldest tennis tournament.

AROUND 750 SCHOOL CHILDREN APPLY FOR THE POSITION OF BALL GIRL AND BALL BOY.

WIMBLEDON IN NUMBERS

£2.2 ($3.1) million prize money for singles champions

11 hours 5 minutes played during the longest match (John Isner vs Nicolas Mahut, 2010)

500,000 spectators in total

166,000 serving of strawberries

10,000 litres (2,199 gallons) of cream

54,250 PRE-TESTED TENNIS BALLS ARE USED DURING THE TOURNAMENT.

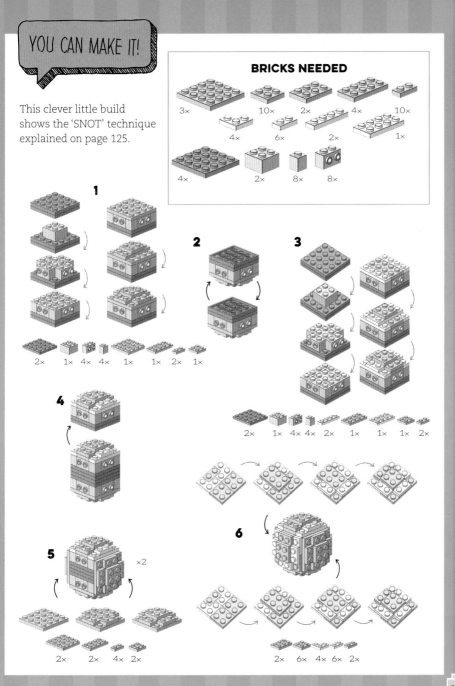

YOU CAN MAKE IT!

This clever little build shows the 'SNOT' technique explained on page 125.

BRICKS NEEDED

3× 10× 2× 4× 10×
4× 6× 2× 1×
4× 2× 8× 8×

1

2× 1× 4× 4× 1× 1× 2× 1×

2

3

2× 1× 4× 4× 2× 1× 1× 1× 2×

4

5

×2

2× 2× 4× 2×

6

2× 6× 4× 6× 2×

Camden Lock

Be prepared for an explosion of colour, sound and activity if you visit Camden. This north London neighbourhood is best known for its colourful, bohemian residents and rock-and-roll music venues. Famous singer Amy Winehouse, with her signature 'beehive' hair-do, was one of its most famous residents.

Colourful Camden

PIRATE CASTLE

Aharrr! There's a pirate castle in the heart of London, and no mistake, Cap'n! It's a sailing club and theatre for children at Camden Lock, and it all began in 1966. Kindly local Lord St David founded the club for mini-pirates to learn to sail and in return they nicknamed him Peg-leg. His cracking canal-based charity continues today in its mock canalside castle.

Alongside Camden Lock – a device for lowering and raising the level of the Regent's Canal – are several huge markets where you can enjoy the spicy scent of international foods and shop for far-out items – from cyberpunk shoes to juggling balls and ice cream frozen using liquid nitrogen!

LOCK

REGENT'S CANAL

Canals once played a vital role in transporting goods across the capital. The Regent's Canal is a 14.5km (9-mile) ribbon of water that runs all the way from Little Venice to the River Thames. The stretch from Little Venice to Camden Town passes beautiful Regent's Park and London Zoo, as well as grand villas designed by architect John Nash.

Granary Square

Behind King's Cross Station, Granary Square is at the heart of a major canal-side redevelopment once full of abandoned warehouses. It has a mesmerising fountain with 1,080 colourfully-lit water jets, which pulse and dance. On hot days the whole area becomes a busy urban beach.

Granary Square

A longboat on Regent's Canal

A HOT TUB WITH A DIFFERENCE

HotTug is the world's first floating hot tub. A cosy fire keeps its waters warm while visitors explore the Regent's Canal nose-to-beak with local ducks.

TURN OVER TO MAKE

CANAL BOAT

This cute model is based on a traditional narrowboat design.

BRICKS NEEDED

1

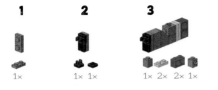

1×

2

1× 1×

3

1× 2× 2× 1×

4

2× 1×

5

1× 1× 6× 1× 1×

6

3× 8×

7

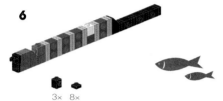

5× 1× 1× 2× 6× 1×

8

1× 1×

9

1× 1× 1× 1× 1× 1×

1×

10

1× 1× 1×

11

1× 1×

12

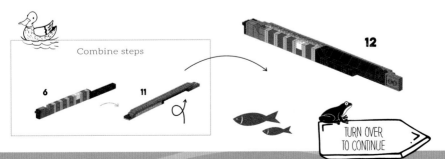

Combine steps

6   11

TURN OVER
TO CONTINUE

CANAL BOAT

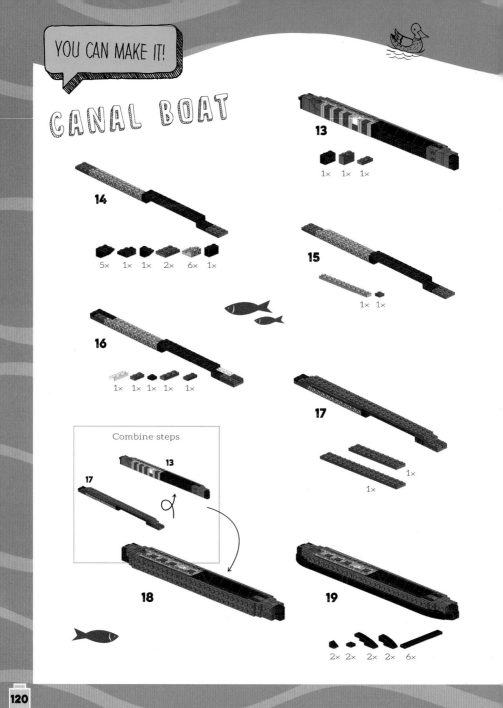

13
1× 1× 1×

14
5× 1× 1× 2× 6× 1×

15
1× 1×

16
1× 1× 1× 1× 1×

Combine steps

17

13

18

17
1×
1×

19
2× 2× 2× 2× 6×

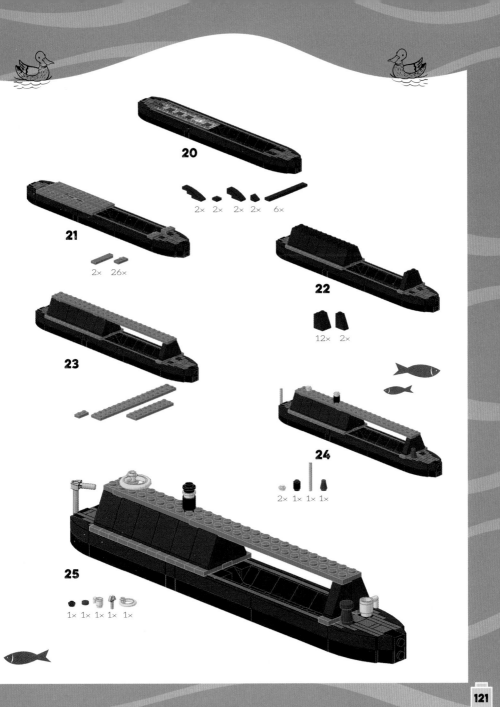

SHERLOCK HOLMES

Sherlock Holmes, the world-famous detective, lived at 221b Baker Street. Inside, the rooms are filled with his Victorian belongings, including his hat, pipes, violin and equipment for solving mysteries.

But hold on a minute...

Holmes was an imaginary character in books written by Sir Arthur Conan Doyle. More than a few fans of the classic detective novels make the trek to this house museum to be greeted by costumed staff.

The Sherlock Holmes Museum

HOLMES DIDN'T REALLY WEAR A DEERSTALKER HAT THAT MUCH!

221B BAKER ST

For years there was a dispute over this famous address, which was actually occupied by Abbey National Bank. A secretary even had the job of responding to fan mail. When the bank moved out, the Royal Mail recognised the museum's right to receive post addressed to Sherlock Holmes.

THE MUSEUM IS ACTUALLY AT NUMBER 239.

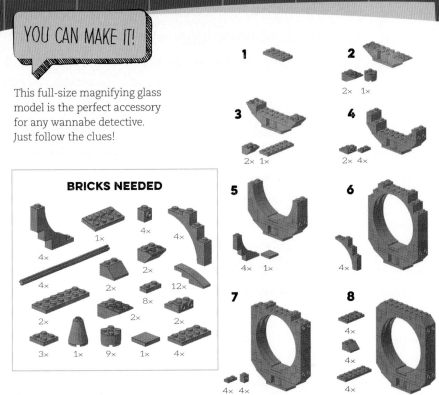

YOU CAN MAKE IT!

This full-size magnifying glass model is the perfect accessory for any wannabe detective. Just follow the clues!

BRICKS NEEDED

10 most useful bricks

These are the most exciting bricks in LEGO®
building. No matter how many of them you
have, there will never quite be enough!

1

2×4 BRICK

The oldest brick
around, this is a
classic. Strong, and
great for adding
structure to
something fragile.

2

1×2 BRACKET

Introduced in 2012,
and so useful! These
pieces help where
other brackets can't
and add real strength
to your models.

3

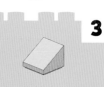

1×1×⅔ SLOPE
(or 'cheese' slope)

A great piece
that gives models
a smooth, modern
look. Useful for
buildings, vehicles
and animals.

4

**1×1 ROUND PLATE
WITH HOLE**

These parts
are perfect for
anchoring rods.

5

TECHNIC PIN JOINER

Structural steelwork
is very important in
architecture and
these pieces joined
together are just the
right shape.

6

1×4 PLATE HINGE

Small but strong
hinges that let you
choose the exact
angle for the pieces
of your creation.

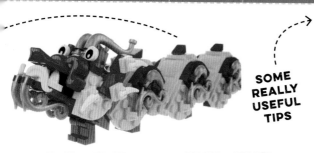

SOME REALLY USEFUL TIPS

BRICKS & PLATES

One LEGO® brick is equal in height to three LEGO® plates. Plates give models more strength (they make great floors), and can incorporate more colour variety and detail in the same space as a brick (see below).

3 = 1 Brick

'SNOT'

It stands for 'Studs Not On Top' – this is a method of turning bricks or plates sideways to make it possible to create quite an accurate curve by turning half of the plates sideways. (see below).

7

1×1 'HEADLIGHT' BRICK

The original 'Studs Not On Top' (SNOT) brick, used for headlights on millions of cars. Its geometry is actually very clever.

8

1×1 BRICK WITH A STUD ON ONE SIDE

These bricks give you a simple way of attaching a plate to the side of a brick. They are used for details or to add a special brick in an unexpected way.

7

1×2 PLATE WITH ONE STUD

(or 'jumper')

When two studs are just too much! Jumpers offset the fine details.

10

1×1 BRICK WITH STUDS ON FOUR SIDES

These are fantastic for creating columns as they can point plates out in four directions.

LEGO® colours

With more than 140 LEGO® colours to choose from, which should you use?

Not all parts exist in all colours, and in fact some very common parts have never been made in some of the obvious colours.

Below and opposite is a guide to some, but not all, of the colours available, using their Bricklink names rather than the official LEGO® ones.

HOW TO FIND THE BRICKS YOU'LL NEED

No matter how many LEGO® bricks anyone has – it's never enough! You don't need to worry if you don't have exactly the same bricks as I've used for these models though. Just try building them with the bricks you have and your imagination!

If you do need to buy more bricks to build some of the models in this book then I've got some tips for you. Did you know you can buy bricks directly from www.lego.com? There is a special section on their online store, just for bricks. Here you can choose from a huge selection of bricks in all sorts of colours to help you build your city. If you're after something very different though, there are special websites allowing people like you to trade bricks? The two best known are www.bricklink.com and www.brickowl.com.

DARK PURPLE   TAN   TRANS-NEON ORANGE   TRANS-PINK

LIGHT YELLOW   DARK BROWN   PINK   TRANS-BLUE

TRANS-GREEN   OLIVE GREEN   PEARL GOLD   TRANS-LIGHT BLUE

CHROME SILVER   BRIGHT LIGHT BLUE   DARK FLESH   LIGHT PURPLE   AQUA

FUN RANGE OF COLOURS

TURQUOISE

SAND BLUE

PEARL LIGHT GREY

PEARL BLACK

BRIGHT YELLOW

TRANS-RED

YELLOW

EARTH ORANGE

VIOLET

DARK RED

TRANS-PURPLE

TRANS-NEON GREEN

SAND GREEN

TRANS-DARK BLUE

TRANS-ORANGE

BRIGHT PINK

DARK BLUISH-GREY

DARK ORANGE

TRANS-CLEAR

REDDISH BROWN

DARK TURQUOISE

TRANS-BLACK

DARK PINK

RED

PEARL SILVER

WHITE

LIGHT BLUISH-GREY

GREEN

DARK AZURE

DARK TAN

PURPLE

MARBLED SILVER

ORANGE

MEDIUM DARK PINK

TRANS-YELLOW

BRIGHT GREEN

BLUE

LIGHT ORANGE

BRIGHT LIGHT YELLOW

DARK GREEN

LIME GREEN

DARK BLUE

MEDIUM BLUE

BLACK

MAERSK BLUE

Acknowledgements

I'd like to thank the other amazing builders who helped to contribute to this book. Rocco Buttliere had already created some amazing LEGO® models of London icons and as they say, there's no point in reinventing the wheel! In addition, my thanks to Alastair Disley, Kirsten Bedigan, Guy Bagley, Tim Johnson, Alex Mallinson and Teresa Elsmore for being instrumental in bringing the book to life!

WE ALWAYS LIKE TO SAY THANK YOU!

Picture Credits

The publisher would like to thank the following for permission to reproduce copyright material

Alamy: p27, 32 (right) Steve Vidler/Mauritius Images GmbH; p27 Richard Bryant/Arcaid Images; p30 Edward Sumner-VIEW; p45 Peter Carroll; p66 Peter Barritt/robertharding; p76 Angelo Hornak; p80 eye35.pix; p106 Marc Tielemans; p.108 PCN Black; p117 Vikram Harish; p122 Gregory Wrona.

Shutterstock.com: p18 (left) Angelina Dimitrova; p18 (right) Dinko G Kyuchukov; p29 Peter Nadoiski; p32 (left) PriceM; p41 Bikeworldtravel; p48 Twocoms; p51 (top) Everett Historical; p51 (bottom) ricochet64; p60 Cedric Weber; p69 DrPhee; p71 Songquan Deng; p74 William Perugini; p96 alice-photo; p102 Chris Jenner; p114 Willy Barton; p116 Ron Ellis.

LEGO Builders: p10 Tate Modern © **Tim Johnson**; p6, 8, 12 Red Phone Box, p14 Globe Theatre, p8, 16 Bowler Hat, p19 Oxo Tower, p20 Battersea Power Station; p8, 23 10 Downing Street, p26 Palace of Westminster, p31 Tower of London, p8, 33 Crown Jewels Orb, p1, 3, 5, 8, 36 Raven, p8, 39 Stocks, p30 Union Jack, p8, 46 Coronation Chair, p49 Fourth Plinth, p4, 8, 52 City of London Dragon, p1, p61 Cleopatra's Needle, p63 Buckingham Palace, p8, 64 Queen's Guard, p68 BT Tower, p9, 71 British Museum, p76 London Monument, p9, 78 Fish and Chips, p81 Borough Market, p3, 9, 83 Food Truck, p89 Afternoon Tea, p9, 91 Chinese Dragon, p96 Covent Garden, p9, 98 Underground Train, p1, 4, 6, 7, 9, 103 Red Bus, p7, 9, 106 Abbey Road, p109 The Orbit, p9, 110 Wicket, p9, 112 Tennis Ball, p144 Camden Lock, p9, 116 Narrow Boat, p5, 9, 122 Magnifying Glass © **Warren Elsmore**; p5, 42 Westminster Abbey, p44 London Eye, p1, 74 The Shard © **Rocco Buttliere**; p66 St Pauls © **Alex M**.

While every effort has been made to credit photographers, The Bright Press would like to apologise should there have been any omissions or errors, and would be pleased to make the appropriate correction for future editions of the book.

ABOUT THE AUTHOR

Warren Elsmore is an artist in LEGO® bricks and a lifelong fan of LEGO®. He is based in Edinburgh, UK. He has been in love with the little bricks since the age of four and is now heavily involved in the LEGO® fan community. Since rediscovering his love of LEGO® at the age of 24, Warren has never looked back. In 2012, after 15 years in a successful IT career, he moved to working full time with LEGO® bricks and now helps many companies to realise their own dreams in plastic. He is the author of several LEGO® books and has organised several international LEGO® conventions.

128